The hungry kitten

Story by Beverley Randell
Illustrated by Leanne Fleming

"Meow, I like this,"
said the hungry little kitten.

3

"Go away," said a big cat.
"Go away, little kitten."

"Meow, I like this,"
said the hungry little kitten.

"Grrr . . . grrr . . . grrr.
Go away," said a big dog.
"Go away, little kitten.
Grrr . . . grrr . . . grrr."

The hungry little kitten
went away.

"Hello, little kitten," said a boy. "Are you hungry?"

"Meow, meow, meow,"
said the hungry little kitten.

"We will take care of you,"
said the boy's mother.

"We like kittens," said the boy.

The little kitten said, "Meow. I like you. I will stay here."